Reflections for a
Special Friend

ISBN: 1 86476 137 7

AXIOM
AUSTRALIA

Reflections for a
Special Friend

AXIOM

The tide of friendship does not rise high on the banks of perfection. Amiable weaknesses and shortcomings are the food of love. It is from the roughness and imperfect breaks in a man that you are able to lay hold of him. ...My friends are not perfect – no more than I – and so we suit each other admirable. It is one of the charitable dispensations of Providence that perfection is not essential to friendship.

Alexander Smith

*T*he right course is to choose for a friend
one who is frank, sociable and sympathetic –
that is, one who is likely to be influenced
by the same motives as yourself –
since all these qualities induce to loyalty …
Since happiness is our best
and highest aim we must, if we would attain it,
give our attention to virtue,
without which we can obtain neither
friendship nor any other desirable thing.

Marcus Tullius Cicero

*T*here are many moments in friendship, as in love,
when silence is beyond words. The faults of our friend may be clear
to us, but it is well to seem to shut our eyes to them.
Friendship is usually treated by the majority of mankind as a
tough and everlasting thing which will survive all manner of bad
treatment. But this is an exceedingly great and foolish error; it may
die in an hour of a single unwise word…

 Marie Louise De La Ramee (Ouida)

*O*nly the person who has faith in himself
Is able to be faithful to others.

*M*eeting interesting people depends less on
Where you go than who you are.

A friend is one to whom one may pour out all the contents of one's heart, chaff and grain together, knowing that the gentlest of hands will take and sift it, keep what is worth keeping and with the breath of kindness blow the rest away.

Arabian Proverb

We inherit our relatives and our features and may not escape them; but we can select our clothing and our friends, and let us be careful that both fit us.

 Volney Streamer

It is a wonderful advantage to a man, in every pursuit or
avocation, to secure an adviser in a sensible woman. In woman
there is at once a subtle delicacy of tact, and a plain soundness of
judgement, which are rarely combined to an equal degree in man.
A woman, if she be really your friend, will have a sensitive regard for
your character, honour, repute.
She will seldom counsel you to do a shabby thing; for a
woman friend always desires to be proud of you.

Sir Edward Bulwer-Lytton

*F*riendship is unnecessary, like philosophy, like art...
It has no survival value;
rather is one of those things that give value to survival.

C S Lewis

*I*f you judge people, you have no time to love them.

Mother Teresa

$\mathscr{P}$romise you won't forget me,
because if I thought you would, I'd never leave.

Winnie the Pooh

$\mathscr{N}$o love, no friendship
Can cross the path of our destiny
Without leaving some mark on it forever.

Francois Mauriac

There are two lasting bequests we can give our children
One is roots
The other is wings.

Hodding Carter Jr.

You will find, as you look back upon your life,
That the moments when you really lived
Are the moments when you have done things in the spirit of love.

Henry Drummond

I've learned that things change,
people change, and it doesn't mean you forget the past
or try to cover it up.
It simple means you move on and treasure the memories.

Alicia Boxer

A good friend is hard to find, hard to lose,
and impossible to forget…

*Y*esterday brought the beginning,
tomorrow brings the end,
but somewhere in the middle we've become best friends.

You can make use of your mistakes, failures, losses, and sufferings. It is not what happens to you so much as what use you make of it. Take your sufferings, difficulties, and hardships and make use of them to help some unfortunate soul who is faced with the same troubles. Then something good will come out of your suffering and the world will be a better place because of it.

The good you do each day will live on, after the trouble and distress have gone, after the difficulty and the pain passed away.

If a friend of mine gave a feast, and did not invite me to it, I should not mind a bit But. if a friend of mine had a sorrow and refused to allow me to share it, I should feel it most bitterly. If he shut the doors of the house of mourning against me, I would move back again and again and beg to be admitted so that I might share in what I was entitled to share. If he thought me unworthy, unfit to weep with him, I should feel it as the most poignant humiliation…

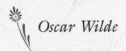 *Oscar Wilde*

$\mathcal{P}$iglet sidled up behind Pooh.

"Pooh," he whispered.

"Yes, Piglet?"

"Nothing," said Piglet, taking Pooh's paw.

"I just wanted to be sure of you."

Winnie the Pooh

$\mathcal{M}$y best friend is my teddy bear,

He never tells my secrets.

I love you not only for what you are,
but for what I am when I am with you.
I love you not only for what you have made of yourself,
but for what you are making of me.
I love you because you have done more than any creed
could have done to make me good, and more than any fate
could have done to make me happy.
You have done it without a touch,
without a word, without a sign.
You have done it by being yourself.
Perhaps that is what being a friend means, after all.

In loneliness, in sickness, in confusion – the mere knowledge of
friendship makes it possible to endure, even if the friend is
powerless to help. It is enough that they exist.
Friendship is not diminished by distance or time, by imprisonment
or war, by suffering or silence.
It is in these things that it roots most deeply.
It is from these things that it flowers.

Pam Brown

$\mathcal{D}$on't walk in front of me, I may not follow.

Don't walk behind me, I may not lead.

Walk beside me and be my friend.

Albert Camus
(also attributed to Maimonidies)

$\mathcal{D}$o not save your loving speeches
For your friends till they are dead;
Do not write them on their tombstones,
Speak them rather now instead.

Anna Cummins

$\mathcal{T}$rust first in those who say –
"I made a mistake."

$\mathcal{Y}$ou must be the change
you wish to see in the world.

Mahatma Gandhi

Take Time

Take time for friendship when you can,
The hours fly swiftly and the need
That presses on your fellow man
May fade away at equal speed,
And you may sigh before the end
That you have failed to play the friend

Not all life's pride is born of fame,
Not all the joy of work is won,
Too late we hang our heads in shame,
Remembering the good we could have done;
Too late we wish that we had stayed
To comfort those who called for aid

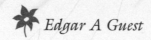 *Edgar A Guest*

$\mathcal{T}$he proper office of a friend is to side with you
when you are wrong.
Nearly anybody will side with you when you are right.

 *Mark Twain*

The more you give, the more you get;
The more you laugh – the less you fret;
The more you do unselfishly
The more you live abundantly.
The more of everything you share
The more you'll always have to spare;
That life is good, and friends are kind.
For only what we give away
Enriches us from day to day.

There are three things that ought to be
Considered before some things are spoken;
The manner,
The place
And the time.

If you think you are beaten, you are;

If you think you dare not, you don't;

If you'd like to win, but think you can't

It's almost a cinch you won't.

If you think you'll lose, you're lost;

For out in the world we find

Success begins with a fellow's will;

It's all in the state of mind.

If you think you are outclassed, you are;

You've got to think high to rise.

You've just got to be sure of yourself

Before you can win the prize.

Life's battles don't always go

To the stronger or faster man,

But sooner or later the man who wins

Is the one who thinks he can.

*T*he severest test of character is not so much the ability to keep a secret as it is, but when the secret is finally out, to refrain from disclosing that you knew it all along.

*W*e cannot tell the precise moment when friendship is formed. As in filling a vessel drop by drop, there is at last a drop which makes it run over; so in a series of kindnesses there is at least one which makes the heart run over.

Samuel Johnson

The glory of friendship is not the outstretched hand, nor the kindly smile, nor the joy of companionship; it is the spiritual inspiration that comes to one when he discovers that someone else believes in him and is willing to trust him with friendship.

Ralph Waldo Emerson

I am not rich and famous
But I do have priceless grandchildren.

*B*e slow in choosing a friend, slower in changing.

Benjamin Franklin

With every friend I love who has been taken into the brown bosom of the earth a part of me has been buried there; but their contribution to my being of happiness, strength and understanding remains to sustain me in an altered world.

 *Helen Keller*

Ten Good Things

There are ten good things
For which no man has ever
Been sorry:—
For doing good to all;
For speaking evil of no one;
For hearing before judging;
For thinking before speaking;
For holding an angry tongue;
For being kind to the distressed;
For asking pardon for all wrongs;
For being patient toward everybody;
For stopping the ear of tale bearer;
For dis-believing most of the evil reports.

$\mathcal{T}$he first ingredient in conversation is truth;
The next, good sense;
The third, good humour;
The fourth, wit.

Sir William Temple

Cherry-O!

If you smile the day will be cheery,
If you smile the day will be bright.
If you think good thoughts you'll be happy,
And everything will work out just right.
So don't let a frown turn you sour,
Don't let bad thoughts make you blue.
Just always remember, think positively,
For how you feel is up to you.

Susan L Wiener

*E*ach of us owes it to our spouse, our children, our friends,
to be as happy as we can be.
And if you don't believe me ask a child what it's like to grow up
with an unhappy parent, or ask parents what suffer if they have an
unhappy child.

Dennis Prager

$\mathcal{I}$ expect to pass through life but once.
If therefore, there can be any kindness I can show,
Or any good thing I can do for any fellow human being,
Let me do it now.
For I shall not pass this way again.

William Penn

The better you know someone, the less there is to say.
Or maybe, there's less that needs to be said.

A smile is a wrinkle that shouldn't be removed.

We all have weaknesses.
But I have figured that
Others have put up with
Mine so tolerantly that
It would be less than fair
Not to make a reasonable
Discount for theirs.

Do more than exist – LIVE
Do more than touch – FEEL
Do more than look – SEE
Do more than hear – LISTEN
Do more than talk – SAY SOMETHING

*L*aughter is the sun that drives the winter from the human face.

Victor Hugo

*P*eople are lonely
Because they Build walls
Instead of bridges.

Joseph Fort Newton

*W*hen you get into a tight place and everything goes against you,
Till it seems as though you could hold on a minute longer,
Never give up then, for that is just the place and time that the tide
will turn.

Harriet Beecher Stoew

*L*ife is not so much what each individual makes of it,
But what we make of it for each other.

*Y*ou can get children off your lap.
But you can never get them out of your heart.

*P*erhaps the most delightful friendships are those in which there is much agreement, much disputation, and yet more personal liking.

George Eliot

A pessimist is someone who feels bad
When she feels good for fear
She will feel worse when she feels better.

*W*hen someone is wronged,
He must put aside all resentment and say
My mind shall not be disturbed
No angry words shall escape my lips
I will remain kind and friendly
With loving thoughts and no secret spite.

Buddhist Prayer

*L*ove has nothing to do with what you are expecting to get
Only with what you are expected to give...

Katherine Hepburn